Mel Bay's

RECORDER

Instruction-Songs-Solos

AF797103

1 2 3 4 5 6 7 8 9 0

CONTENTS

MEL BAY ®

PARTS OF THE RECORDER

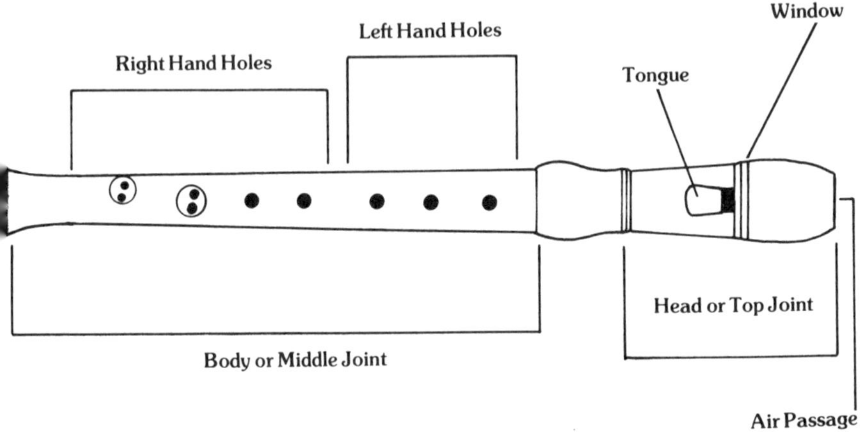

4 HOW TO HOLD THE RECORDER

TYPES OF NOTES

	THE TYPE OF NOTE WILL INDICATE THE LENGTH OF ITS SOUND.

 THIS IS A WHOLE NOTE.

= 4 BEATS
A WHOLE-NOTE WILL RECEIVE FOUR BEATS OR COUNTS.

 THIS IS A HALF NOTE.

 = 2 BEATS
A HALF-NOTE WILL RECEIVE TWO BEATS OR COUNTS.

 THIS IS A QUARTER NOTE.

 = 1 BEAT
A QUARTER NOTE WILL RECEIVE ONE BEAT OR COUNT.

 THIS IS AN EIGHTH NOTE

 = ½ BEAT
AN EIGHTH-NOTE WILL RECEIVE ONE-HALF BEAT OR COUNT. (2 FOR 1 BEAT)

 THIS IS A SIXTEENTH NOTE.

 = ¼ BEAT — 4 PER BEAT

RESTS

A REST is a sign to designate a period of silence. This period of silence will be of the same duration as the note to which it corresponds.

 THIS IS AN EIGHTH REST

 THIS IS A SIXTEENTH REST

 THIS IS A QUARTER REST

 THIS IS A HALF REST
Note that it lays on the line.

 THIS IS A WHOLE REST
Note that it hangs down from the line.

NOTES

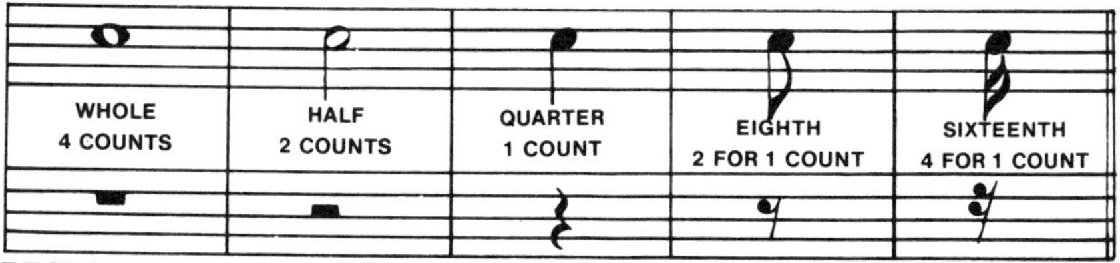

RESTS

THE TIME SIGNATURE

The above examples are the common types of time signatures to be used in this book.

4 The top number indicates the number of beats per measure

4 The bottom number indicates the type of note receiving one beat beats per measure

4 beats per measure

4 a quarter-note receives one beat.

6 BEATS PER MEASURE

8 EACH EIGHTH-NOTE RECEIVES ONE FULL BEAT
(See p. 26 & 27)

Signifies so called "common time" and is simply another way of designating $\frac{4}{4}$ time.

BASIC FINGERING CHART

● = Finger pressed down over hole
○ = Open hole
◒ = Partially closed hole

Thumb Hole (in back)

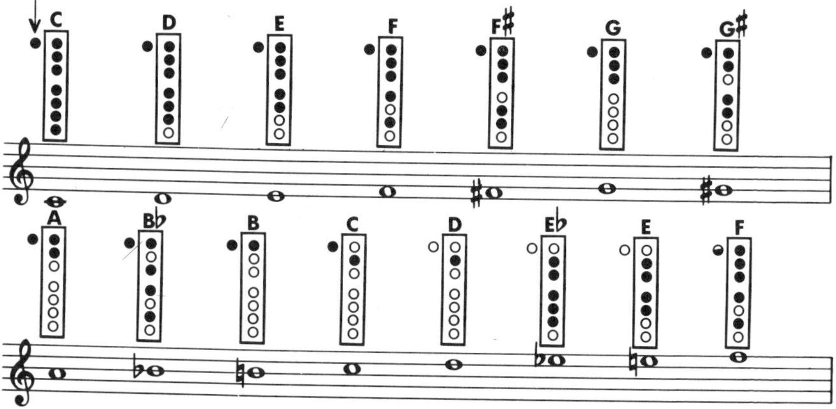

NOTES TO BE USED

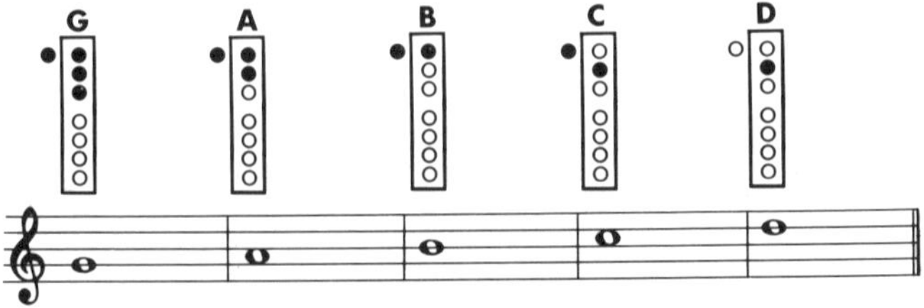

CLIMBING

STAIRCASE

MORE NEW NOTES

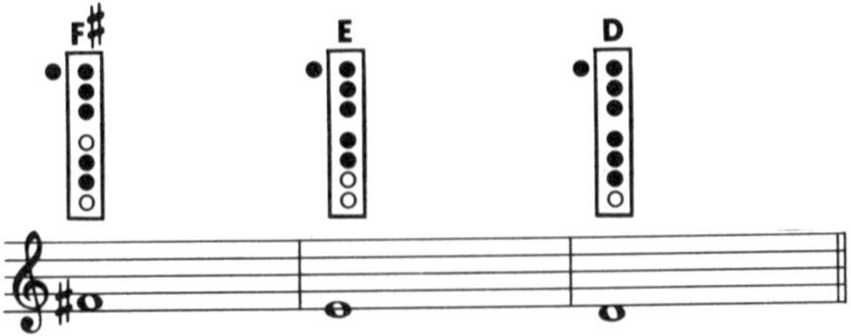

NEW NOTE STUDY

NEW NOTES TO BE USED

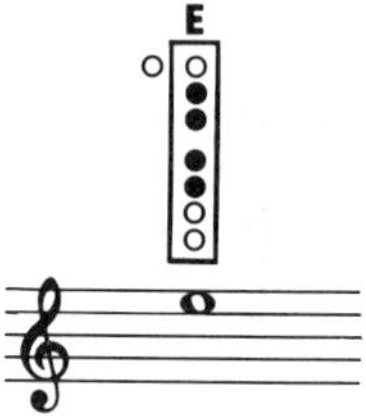

BROTHER JOHN

AU CLAIR DE LUNE #1

Repeat Sign - means to go back to beginning

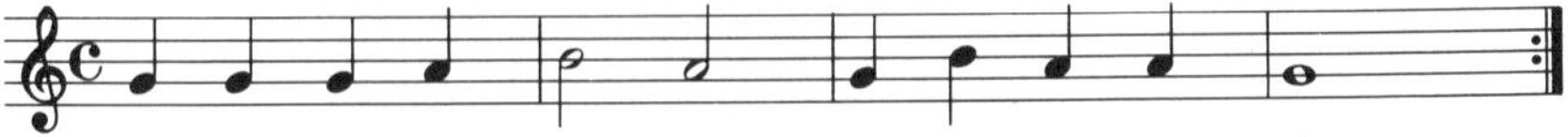

AU CLAIR DE LUNE #2

DOTTED QUARTER NOTES

A DOT AFTER A NOTE increases its Value by ONE-HALF.

The count for the dotted quarter-note is as follows:

ALL THROUGH THE NIGHT

SLUR

A slur looks like this:

To slur, tongue the 1st note and then finger only (Don't Tongue) the succeeding notes.

Dotted Half Note

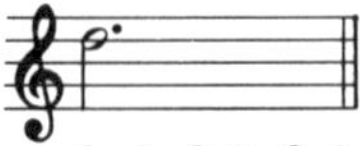

Count: 1 & 2 & 3 &

SLUR SONG

TELL ME WHY

ALOUETTE

KEY SIGNATURE

KEY OF G

F Sharp in the Key Signature means you are in the key of G. All F's will be sharped (F ♯) unless they have a Natural Sign (F ♮)

THE TIE

A tie connects two or more notes of the same pitch.
When a tie occurs, only the 1st note is tongued. The following notes are held.

TIE SONG

NOBODY KNOWS THE TROUBLE I'VE SEEN

20 FIRST AND SECOND ENDING

Sometimes in music 2nd endings are needed.

The 1st leads back to the beginning and the 2nd ending either ends the piece or leads on into the following section.

I'VE GOT PEACE LIKE A RIVER

CAMPTOWN RACES

GRANDFATHER'S CLOCK

PRAISE HIM IN THE MORNING

F NATURAL AND LOW C

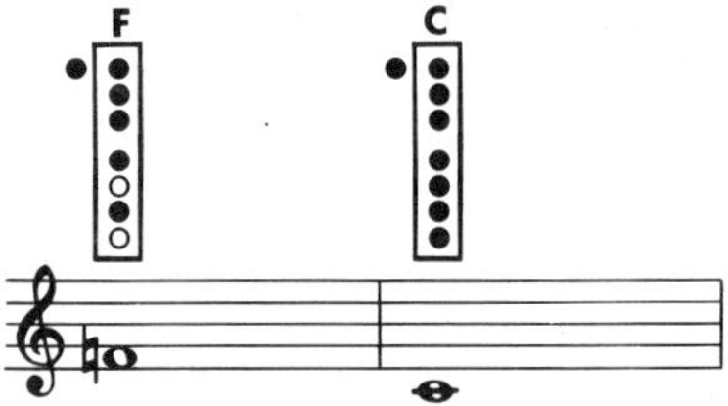

NEW NOTE SONG

OH, SUSANNA

CHESTER

AMAZING GRACE

WHEN JOHNNY COMES MARCHING HOME

IRISH WASHERWOMAN

RIDDLE SONG

JACOB'S LADDER

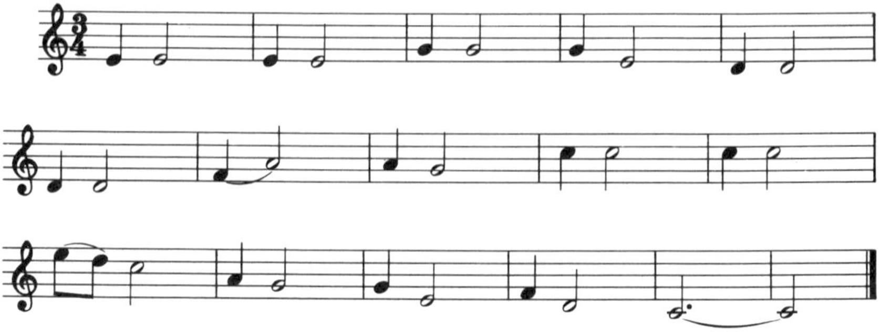

ANOTHER NEW NOTE

F

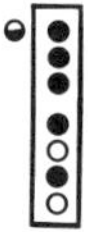

Remember, with F, the thumb hole is only partially covered. Listen carefully for the correct pitch.

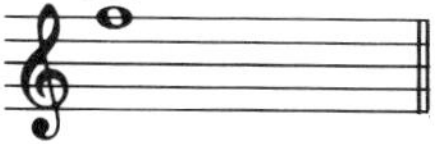

AURA LEE